Implementing Information Security based on ISO 27001 / ISO 27002 - A Management Guide

Other publications by Van Haren Publishing

Van Haren Publishing (VHP) specializes in titles on Best Practices, methods and standards within four domains:
- IT management,
- Architecture (Enterprise and IT),
- Business management and
- Project management

These publications are grouped in series: *ITSM Library, Best Practice* and *IT Management Topics*. VHP is also publisher on behalf of leading companies and institutions:
The Open Group, IPMA-NL, PMI-NL, CA, Getronics, Quint, The Sox Institute and ASL BiSL Foundation

Topics are (per domain):

IT (Service) Management / IT Governance	Architecture (Enterprise and IT)	Project/Programme/ Risk Management
ASL	Archimate®	A4-Projectmanagement
BiSL	GEA®	ICB / NCB
CATS	TOGAF™	MINCE®
CMMI		M_o_R®
CobiT	**Business Management**	MSP
ISO 17799	EFQM	PMBoK®
ISO 27001	ISA-95	PRINCE2®
ISO/IEC 20000	ISO 9000	
ISPL	ISO 9001:2000	
IT Service CMM	SixSigma	
ITIL® V2	SOX	
ITIL® V3	SqEME®	
ITSM		
MOF		
MSF		
ABC of ICT		

For the latest information on VHP publications, visit our website: www.vanharen.net.

Implementing
Information Security
based on
ISO 27001/ISO 27002
A Management Guide

Colophon

Title:	Implementing Information Security based on ISO 27001/ISO 27002 - A Management Guide
Series:	Best Practice
Lead Author:	Alan Calder
Chief Editor:	Jan van Bon
Publisher:	Van Haren Publishing, Zaltbommel, www.vanharen.net
ISBN:	978 90 8753 541 4
Print:	First edition, first impression, May 2006 First edition, second impression, November 2007 First edition, third impression, January 2009 Second edition, first impression, July 2009
Design and Layout:	CO2 Premedia, Amersfoort – NL
Copyright:	© Van Haren Publishing 2009

This title was updated in 2009 to reflect changes made to the Standard in 2008.

Permission to reproduce extracts of BS ISO/IEC 27001: 2005 (BS 7799-2: 2005) is granted by BSI. British Standards can be obtained from BSI Customer Services, 389 Chiswick High Road, London W4 4AL. Tel: +44 (0)20 8996 9001. email: cservices@bsi-global.com

For any further enquiries about Van Haren Publishing, please send an e-mail to: info@vanharen.net

Aknowledgements

Van Haren Publishing would like to thank Alan Calder, the lead author, for his expert, flexible approach and his professional delivery.

Title: Implementing Information Security based on ISO 27001/ ISO 27002
              A Management Guide

Lead Author: Alan Calder

Editors: Jan van Bon (Inform-IT), Chief Editor
           Selma Polter, Editor

Review Team: Dr Gary Hinson   IsecT
             Steve G Watkins, HMCPSI (UK Government:
                               Crown Prosecution Service Inspectorate)
             Dr Jon G. Hall   Centre for Research in Computing,
                               The Open University

Contents

CHAPTER 1

Introduction

This Management Guide provides an overview of the implementation of an Information Security Management System that conforms to the requirements of ISO/IEC 27001:2005 and which uses controls derived from ISO/IEC 27002:2005. This book is intended as a companion to the *Management Guide on ISO 27001& ISO 27002*, so it repeats very little of that book's information about the background and components of the two information security standards. It is an overview of implementation, rather than a detailed implementation guide, and it is not a substitute for reading and studying the two Standards themselves.

1.1   ISO/IEC 27001:2005 ('ISO 27001' or 'the Standard')

This is the most recent, most up-to-date, international version of a standard specification for an Information Security Management System. It is vendor-neutral and technology-independent. It is designed for use in organizations of all sizes ('intended to be applicable to all organizations, regardless of type, size and nature'[1]) and in every sector (e.g. 'commercial enterprises, government agencies, not-for-profit organizations'[2]), anywhere in the world. It is a management system, not a technology specification and this is reflected in its formal title, which is "Information Technology - Security Techniques - Information Security Management Systems - Requirements." ISO 27001 is also the first of a series of international information security standards, all of which will have ISO 27000 numbers.

1.2   ISO/IEC 27002:2005 ('ISO 27002')

This Standard is titled "Information Technology - Security Techniques - Code of Practice for information security management." Published in July 2005, it replaced ISO/IEC 17799:2000, which has now been withdrawn. This Standard now has the number ISO/IEC 27002, in order to clarify that it belongs to the ISO/IEC 27000 family of standards.

1.3 Definitions

ISO 27001 defines an ISMS, or Information Security Management System, as 'that part of the overall management system, based on a business risk approach, to establish, implement, operate, monitor, review, maintain and improve information security. The management system includes organizational structure, policies, planning activities, responsibilities, practices, procedures, processes and resources.'

Other definitions are intended to be consistent with those used in related information security standards, such as ISO/IEC 27006:2005, ISO/IEC 27005:2007 et cetera.

An ISMS needs a consistent set of definitions, so that there is a consistent understanding of its requirements across all those who are within its scope. The definitions of ISO 27001 should be adopted, supported where necessary by additional definitions from ISO 27002.

---

1) ISO/IEC 27001:2005 Application 1.2
2) ISO/IEC 27001:2005 Scope 1.1

CHAPTER 2

Information security and ISO 27001

Effective information security is defined in the Standard as the 'preservation of confidentiality, integrity and availability of information.'[3] It cannot be achieved through technological means alone, and should never be implemented in a way that is either out of line with the organization's approach to risk or which undermines or creates difficulties for its business operations.

2.1 Approach to information security

The ISMS includes 'organizational structure, policies, planning activities, responsibilities, practices, procedures, processes and resources'[4] and is a structured, coherent management approach to information security. It should be designed to ensure the effective interaction of the three key attributes of information security:

- process (or procedure);
- technology;
- behavior.

The decision to develop an ISMS should be a strategic business decision. It should be debated, agreed and driven by the organization's board of directors or equivalent top management group. The design and implementation of the ISMS should be directly influenced by the organization's 'needs and objectives, security requirements, the processes employed and the size and structure of the organization.'[5]

2.2 The ISMS and organizational needs

ISO 27001 is not a one-size-fits-all solution to an organization's information security management needs. It should not interfere with the growth and development of the business. According to ISO 27001:

---

3) ISO/IEC 27001:2005 Terms and Definitions 3.4
4) ISO/IEC 27001:2005 Terms and Definitions 3.7 Note
5) ISO/IEC 27001:2005 Introduction General 0.1

- the ISMS 'will be scaled in accordance with the needs of the organization'
- a 'simple situation requires a simple ISMS solution';
- the ISMS is 'expected to change over time';
- the Standard is meant to be a useful model for 'establishing, implementing, operating, monitoring, reviewing, maintaining and improving an ISMS.'[6]

It is a model that can be applied anywhere in the world, and understood anywhere in the world. It is also technology-neutral and can be implemented in any hardware or software environment.

2.3 Reasons to implement an ISMS

There are, broadly, four reasons for an organization to implement an ISMS:
- *strategic* - a government or parent company requirement, or a strategic board decision, to better manage its information security within the context of its overall business risks;
- *customer confidence* - the need to demonstrate to one or more customers that the organization complies with information security management best practice, or the opportunity to gain a competitive edge, in customer and supplier relationships, over its competitors;
- *regulatory* - the desire to meet various statutory and regulatory requirements, particularly around computer misuse, data protection and personal privacy;
- *internal effectiveness* - the desire to manage information more effectively within the organization.

While all four of these reasons for adopting an ISMS are good ones, it must be remembered that having an ISO 27001-compliant ISMS will not automatically 'in itself' confer immunity from legal obligations.' The organization will have to ensure that it understands the range of legislation and regulation with which it must comply, ensure that these requirements are reflected in the ISMS as it is developed and implemented, and then ensure that the ISMS works as designed.

As figure 2.1 illustrates, an ISMS potentially enables an organization to deliver against all four of these objectives.

---

6) All 4 quotes from ISO/IEC 27001:2005 Introduction General 0.1
7) ISO/IEC 27001:2005 Title Note

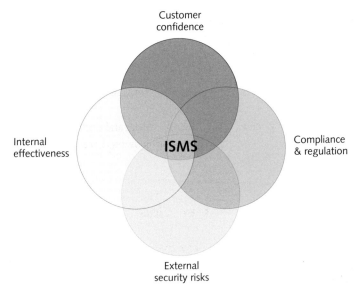

Figure 2.1 *Strategic information risk management*

2.4 The ISMS and regulation

Regulations and the law in each of the areas mentioned above are still evolving; they are sometimes poorly drafted, often contradictory (particularly between jurisdictions) and have little or no case law to provide guidance for organizations in planning their compliance efforts. It can be difficult for organizations to identify specific methods for complying with individual laws. In these circumstances, implementation of a best practice ISMS may, in legal proceedings, support a defense in court that the management did everything that was reasonably practicable for it to do in meeting its legal and regulatory requirements. Of course, every organization would have to take its own legal advice on issues such as this and neither this book nor this author provides guidance of any sort on this issue.

As figure 2.2 demonstrates, an ISMS enables an organization to meet existing, clearly defined regulatory compliance requirements as well as those that are still emergent and are either unclear or untested.

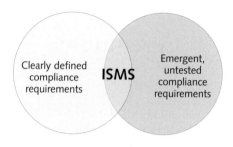

Figure 2.2 *The ISMS and regulation*

CHAPTER 3

Certification

ISO/IEC 27001:2005 is a specification for an ISMS. It is not a set of guidelines or a Code of Practice. Any organization that implements an ISMS which it wishes to have assessed against the Standard will have to follow the specification contained in the Standard. As a general rule, organizations implementing an ISMS based on ISO/IEC 27001:2005 will need to pay close attention to the wording of the Standard itself, and to be aware of any revisions to it. Non-compliance with any official revisions, which usually occur on a three-year and a five-year cycle, will jeopardize an existing certification.

3.1 Read and study the Standards

The Standard itself is what an ISMS will be assessed against; where there is any conflict between advice provided in this or any other guide to implementation of ISO 27001 and the Standard itself, it is the wording in the Standard that should be heeded. An external certification auditor will be assessing the ISMS against the published Standard, not against the advice provided by this book, a sector scheme manager, a consultant or any other third party. It is critical that those responsible for the ISMS should be able to refer explicitly to its clauses and intent and be able to defend any implementation steps they have taken against the Standard itself.

An appropriate first step is to obtain and read copies of ISO/IEC 27001:2005 and ISO/IEC 27002:2005. Copies can be purchased from the ISO website, from national standards bodies and from www.itgovernance.co.uk; standards should be available in hard copy and downloadable versions.

ISO 27001 provides a specification against which an organization's ISMS can be independently audited by an accredited certification body. If the ISMS is found to conform to the specification, the organization can be issued with a formal certificate confirming this.

3.2 'Badge on the wall' debate

There are two approaches to implementation of the Standard:
- develop and implement an ISMS to meet the requirements of the Standard and have it certificated;
- develop and implement an ISMS but do not seek certification.

This is known as 'the badge on the wall' debate.

The argument in favor of certification is, in essence, that this route enables other organizations (customers, partners and suppliers) to obtain, without having to carry out their own audit, a level of reassurance about the effectiveness and completeness of the ISMS. It can also be presented as evidence of compliance with many aspects of information-related regulation.

The argument against is that a 'badge on the wall' is not necessary to prove to the organization that its ISMS is adequate or that it is doing a good job of preserving information security.

ISO 27001 is drafted, as is all guidance on implementation, on the assumption that the organization implementing an ISMS ISO 27001 will seek certification; ISO 27002 provides guidance for organizations that simply wish to develop an ISMS that uses best practice controls. Any organization that claims it has an ISO 27001-compliant ISMS but which has not subjected itself to certification should, under the risk assessment requirements of the Standard, be treated like any other organization that *does not have an adequate information security management system* - until proven otherwise.

Four broad reasons were identified, in the previous chapter, for implementing an ISO 27001-conforming ISMS. While two of them (customer confidence and regulatory best practice demonstration) can only be achieved through certification, the other two could perhaps be achieved without.

However, as most people recognize, independent third party verification has a reliable track record in helping organizations make a success of almost any initiative.

Third party certification is an absolute necessity for any ISO 27001 ISMS; not only does it give management and the business an initial, as well as an ongoing, target at which to aim, but it also ensures that the Standard is properly understood and effectively implemented.

3.3 Certification

The *Management Guide to ISO27001 & ISO27002* provides an overview of the certification process and the Standards under which accredited certification auditors are required to operate.

3.4 Qualifications and further study

It is an expectation of ISO 27001 that its implementation will be in the hands of qualified people. Appropriate qualifications can be obtained in a number of ways, included through the UK Open University's information Security course and the British Computer Society's ISEB information security qualification. In addition, many certification bodies offer ISO 27001 lead auditor training courses.

Practitioners should also keep themselves up-to-date with current developments within the information security field, both through industry journals and magazines, and through relevant industry websites, such as www.itgovernance.co.uk/iso27001.aspx.

CHAPTER 4
ISO 27001 and ISO 27002

It is important to understand the relationship between the two information security Standards.

4.1 ISO 27002

ISO/IEC 27002:2005 is a **Code of Practice**. It provides **guidance** and uses words like *'may'* and *'should'*. It provides an internationally accepted framework for best practice in Information Security Management and systems interoperability. It also provides guidance on how to implement an ISMS capable of certification, to which an external auditor could refer. It does not provide the basis for an international certification scheme.

4.2 ISO 27001

ISO/IEC 27001:2005 is a **specification** for an ISMS. It sets out **requirements** and uses words like *'must'* and *'shall'*. One mandatory requirement is that 'control objectives and controls from Annex A shall be selected' in order to meet the 'requirements identified by the risk assessment and risk treatment process.'[8] Annex A to ISO/IEC 27001:2005 lists the 133 controls that are in ISO/IEC 27002:2005, follows the same numbering system as that Standard and uses the same words and definitions.

As the preface to ISO 27001 states, 'the control objectives and controls referred to in this edition are directly derived from and aligned with those listed in ISO/IEC 27002:2005.'[9] ISO 27002, though, provides substantial implementation guidance on how individual controls should be approached. Anyone implementing an ISO 27001 ISMS will need to acquire and study copies of both ISO 27001 and ISO 27002.

While ISO 27001 in effect mandates the use of ISO 27002 as a source of guidance on controls, control selection and control implementation, it does not limit the organization's choice of controls to those in ISO 27002. The preface goes on to state: 'The list of control objectives and controls in this ISO Standard is not exhaustive and an organization might consider that additional control objectives and controls are necessary.'[10]

---

8) ISO/IEC 27001:2005 4.2.1 g) Select control objectives and controls for the treatment of risks
9) ISO/IEC 27001:2005 Preface
10) Ibid.

CHAPTER 5

Frameworks and management system integration

ISO 27001 is designed to harmonise with ISO 9001:2008 and ISO 14001:2004. This makes it possible to develop a completely integrated management system that can achieve certification to ISO 27001, ISO 9001 and ISO 14001.

'It is essential that your ISMS is fully integrated into your organization; it will not work effectively if is a separate management system and exists outside of and parallel to any other management systems. Logically, this means that the framework, processes and controls of the ISMS must, to the greatest extent possible, be integrated with, for instance, your ISO 9001 quality system; you want one document control system, you want one set of processes for each part of the organization, etc. Clearly, therefore, assessment of your management systems must also be integrated: you only want one audit, which deals with all the aspects of your management system. It is simply too disruptive of the organization, too costly and too destructive of good business practice, to do anything else.'[11]

There are significant cost benefits to be obtained from this sort of streamlining; these come in addition to the significantly more important benefits that are derived from improving the focus and cohesiveness of the organization's quality assurance activities.

5.1   ITIL

ITIL (the IT Infrastructure Library) is a set of best practices at the heart of IT service management. The most recent version is ITILv3, the IT Lifecycle Management Process. ITILv2 includes one manual titled 'Best Practice for Security Management', which was written and published in 1999. This manual aligns with **BS7799:1995**, although it also took BS7799:1999 (draft) into account. This means that it was written before the publication of BS7799 as a two-part standard and is aligned with what is now ISO 17799, although the version with which it is aligned has now been updated twice.

The manual's starting point is existing ITIL processes, to which it then adds security processes. Although it is technically out-of-date, it still supplies extremely useful guidance to any organization that treats any part of its IT operation as a 'service', particularly if that service is the subject of an SLA, whether internal or external.

---

11) IT Governance: a Manager's Guide to Data Security and ISO27001/ISO27002 (4th edition), Alan Calder and Steve Watkins, published by Kogan Page 2008, page 338

5.2 ISO 20000

ISO/IEC 20000-1 is the Standard that specifies best practice for IT service management, and is the specification for IT service management against which an organization's actual practices can be certified.

Clause 6.6 of ISO 20000-1 deals with information security. It cross-refers to ISO 27002. It requires:

- management to approve an information security policy
- communicating it to all relevant personnel and customers;
- selecting security controls on the basis of a risk assessment;
- implementing and operating appropriate security controls;
- including security in third party agreements;
- implementing an information security incident management procedure;
- measuring and monitoring information security activities;
- planning to improve information security.

Clearly, these requirements are best met by implementing an information security management system that conforms to ISO 27001.

Any organization that is pursuing ISO 20000 should think through, before project initiation, how it will integrate these two management systems. There is already some commonality between the two and, while information security is treated as an important aspect of IT service management, IT service management is also treated as an important area in information security.

5.3 ISO 27001 Annex C

Annex C to ISO 27001 (which is informative, not mandatory - no organization is required to try and integrate its management systems) shows how its individual clauses correspond to the clauses of ISO 9001:2008 and ISO 14001:2004.

While Annex C includes the correspondence with ISO 14001:2004, table 5.1 shows instead the correspondences between ISO 27001, ISO 9001 and ISO 20000-1:2005.

ISO 27001:2005		ISO 9001:2008		ISO 20000-1:2005	
4	Information Security Management System	4	Quality Management System	3	Requirements for a management system
4.1	General requirements			4	Planning and implementing service management
4.2	Establishing and managing the ISMS	4.1	General requirements		
4.2.1	Establish the ISMS			4.1	Plan service management
4.2.2	Implement & operate the ISMS				
				4.2	Implement service management and provide the services
4.2.3	Monitor and review the ISMS	8.2.3	Monitoring and measurement of processes	4.3	Monitoring, measuring and reviewing
		8.2.4	Monitoring and measurement of product		
4.2.4	Maintain & improve the ISMS			4.4	Continual improvement
				3.2	Documentation
4.3	Documentation requirements	4.2	Documentation requirements		requirements
4.3.1	General	4.2.1	General		
		4.2.2	Quality manual		
4.3.2	Control of documents	4.2.	Control of documents		
4.3.3	Control of records	4.2.4	Control of records		
5	Management responsibility	5	Management responsibility	3.1	Management responsibility
5.1	Management commitment	5.1	Management commitment		
		5.2	Customer focus	4.4.1	Policy
		5.3	Quality policy		
		5.4	Planning		
		5.5	Responsibility, authority and communication		
5.2	Resource management	6	Resource management		
5.2.1	Provision of resources	6.1	Provision of resources		
		6.2	Human resources		
5.2.2	Training, awareness and competence	6.2.2	Competence, awareness and training	3.3	Competence, awareness and training
		6.3	Infrastructure		
		6.4	Work environment		
6	Internal ISMS audits	8.2.2	Internal audit	Included in 4.3	
7	Management review of the ISMS	5.6	Management review		
		5.6.1	General		
7.1	General	5.6.2	Review input		
7.2	Review input	5.6.3	Review output		
7.3	Review output				
8	ISMS improvement	8.5	Improvement	4.4.2	Management of improvements
8.1	Continual improvement	8.5.1	Continual improvement		
8.2	Corrective action				
8.3	Preventive action	8.5.2	Corrective action		
		8.5.3	Preventive action		

Table 5.1 *Correspondences between ISO 27001, ISO 9001 and ISO 20000-1:2005*

5.4 Management system integration

For many organizations, the critical correspondences will be between ISO 27001 and ISO 9001 and it is in the areas of obvious overlap that the integration of management systems starts. Practically speaking, the most important overlaps are:
- Clause 4.3, which deals with documentation requirements;
- Clause 5.1, which deals with management commitment;
- Clause 7, which deals with management review;
- Clause 8, which deals with management system improvement;
- Clause 6, which deals with internal audits.

What these clauses make possible between them is the deployment of common documentation, management and audit processes for both management systems. For instance, the organization only needs a single management system that incorporates its quality and its information security procedures, a single comprehensive and integrated audit process that covers all aspects of its activity, and a standard management authorization, approval, monitoring, review and quality improvement process that deals with all its activities irrespective of whether they fall within the scope of the information security management system, the quality management system or the environmental management system.

The note to Clause 1.2 of ISO 27001 recognizes this simple principle: 'If an organization already has an operative business process management system, it is preferable in most cases to satisfy the requirements of this International Standard within this existing management system.'

5.5 BS25999

BS25999 provides a specification for a business continuity framework that can make a significant contribution to the development of the business continuity plan(s) that are specified as being required in Clause A. 14 of the Annex to ISO 27001 (for medium and large organizations and often for smaller ones). ISO 27001 pre-supposes the existence of a business continuity plan.

The only formal standard to which organizations can turn is BS25999. It makes practical sense for an organization to seek guidance on such a mission-critical subject from a standard such as this. Copies of BS25999 can be obtained from BSI and from other standards distributors.

BS25999 uses terms that will be familiar to those developing an ISMS, including 'risk assessment' and 'impacts'. The principle that ought to be applied is that, where there is any gap between the requirements of ISO 27001 (including in definitions, process, etc) and the guidance of BS25999, it is ISO 27001 that must have primacy. A business continuity framework developed in line with BS25999 will certainly be adequate to the requirements of an information security management system and will be capable of supporting the information security control requirements of ISO 27001's Clause A.14.

5.6 CobiT

CobiT, or Control Objectives for Information and related Technology (now in version 4.1), is 'a model for the control of the IT environment.'[13] While this book is not about CobiT, anyone deploying an ISO 27001 ISMS should be aware of it. The *Management Guide to ISO 27001& ISO 27002* includes a chapter on the relationship between ISO 27001 and CobiT.
The key areas of correspondence between ISO 27001 and CobiT are shown in table 5.2.

ISO 27001		CobiT 4.1	
4.2.1.a & b	Define ISMS scope and policy	PO6	Communicate management aims and direction
4.2.1.c et seq	Risk assessment	PO9	Assess and manage IT risks
4.2.2.e and 5.2.2.	Training and awareness	DS7	Educate and train users
4.2.2.f	Manage operations	DS13	Manage operations
4.2.2.h & 8	Security incidents and continuous improvement	DS10	Manage problems and incidents
4.2.3	Monitor and review	ME1	Monitor & evaluate IT performance & ME2 Monitor & evaluate internal control
4.3	Documentation requirements	PO4	Define the IT processes
6	Internal ISMS audits	ME2	Monitor & evaluate internal control

Table 5.2 *Key areas of correspondence between ISO 27001 and CobiT*

---

13) IT Governance based on CobiT: A Management Guide, Van Haren Publishing 2004, page 23

CHAPTER 6

Documentation requirements and record control

When implementing an ISMS, organizations are attempting to institutionalize some of the knowledge and behavior that is required for the management of their information security in a way that will be both repeatable and secure against the possibility that critical knowledge might be lost when an individual leaves the organization. Repeatable processes are more consistent, and more predictable. Every management system depends for its effectiveness on proper documentation of its processes and the retention of records that demonstrate compliance or non-conformance with the system.

As part of its longer-term programme of continuous improvement, organizations should look to Capability Maturity Models[14] to provide them with guidance on how they can strengthen and improve the processes that make up their ISMS.

Control A. 10.1.1 explicitly requires security procedures to be documented, maintained and made available to all users who need them. A compliant ISMS will be fully documented. However, not every organization has to implement an equally complex documentation structure. 'The extent of the ISMS documentation can differ from one organization to another owing to the size of the organization and the type of its activities and the scope and complexity of the security requirements and the system being managed.'[15]

6.1 ISO 27001 Document control requirements

Clause 4.3.2 of ISO 27001 deals with the documentation requirements for the ISMS. Firstly, all documents need to be controlled. This means that they must:

- be approved (or reviewed and re-approved) before use;
- have a current revision and issue status (e.g. draft, final, and a version number);
- have an issue date;
- identify the document owner;
- record the change history of the document;
- be available at all points of use;

14) IT Service CMM, a pocket guide, van Haren, 2004

15) ISO/IEC 27001:2005 4.3.1 note 2

- be legible, readily identifiable and stored or used in line with their classification (see below);
- be withdrawn when obsolete;
- be appropriately identified if their origin is external to the organization.

6.2 Annex A document controls

There are document-related controls in Annex A that should also be included in the document control aspects of the ISMS. They are all important controls in their own right; they are:

- A.7.2.1 Classification guidelines, which deal with confidentiality levels, and which mean that every document should be marked with its confidentiality classification;
- A.7.2.2 Information labeling and handling, which deals with how confidentiality levels are marked on information and information media;
- A.15.1.4 Data protection and privacy of personal information, which may affect who is entitled to see what information.

6.3 Document approval

The issue of controlled documents must be approved as adequate, as will any revisions. Approval must be from an appropriate level of authority and should represent the ISO 27001 requirement (A.10.1.3) for segregation of duties: the person who drafts a document should not be responsible for the final approval before its release. Practically, one has to allow for revision and improvement to documents; those that are most detailed are prone to change most frequently as process improvements are identified. It makes sense for those documents that are likely to be frequently revised to be approved at the lowest possible level within the organization.

The way to do this is to create a tiered document structure, in which those documents which undergo only infrequent change are subject to the most senior level of approval, while those likely to change frequently are subject to a much lower level of sign-off.

Policies, which set general direction and requirements, should not need to change frequently, and should be subject to board (or other top management) approval. Procedures, which implement policy, are likely to change from time to time, and should be subject to middle management approval (by the person ultimately responsible for the department or process to which the procedure applies). Work instructions, which set out the detailed, step-by-step requirements for carrying out specific functions, should be subject to approval by the person to whom the relevant asset owner reports.

Figure 6.1 shows a typical four-tier documentation structure.

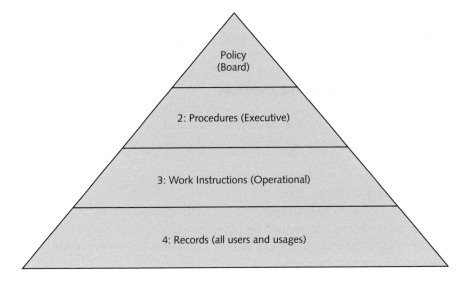

Figure 6.1 *Typical documentation structure*

6.4 Contents of the ISMS documentation

Documentation has to be complete, comprehensive, in line with the requirements of the Standard and tailored to suit the needs of individual organizations. ISO27001 describes (in Clause 4.3.1) the minimum documentation that should be included in the ISMS in order to meet the requirement that the organization maintains sufficient records to demonstrate compliance with the requirements of the Standard. These documents include:

- the information security policy, the scope statement for the ISMS, the risk assessment methodology and output of the risk assessment exercise, the various control objectives and procedures that support the ISMS, and the statement of applicability. Together, these form the ISMS manual;
- evidence of the actions undertaken by the organization and its management to specify the scope of the ISMS (the minutes of board and steering committee meetings, as well as any specialist reports). The Standard requires that there should be records of management decisions, that all actions should be traceable to these decisions and policies, and that any results that have been recorded should be reproducible;

- a description of the management framework (project team/steering committee, etc). This could usefully be related to an organizational structure chart;
- the risk treatment plan and the underpinning, documented procedures (which should include responsibilities and required actions) that implement each of the specified controls. A procedure describes who has to do what, under what conditions, or by when, and how. The Standard also requires that the relationship between the selected control, the results of the risk assessment and the risk treatment process, and the ISMS policy and objectives, should all be demonstrable;
- the procedures (which should include responsibilities and required actions) that govern the management and review of the ISMS.

6.5 Record control

Records have to be kept, as required by ISO 27001 Clause 4.3.3, to provide evidence that the ISMS conforms to the requirements of the Standard. There are not the same as the records that the organization has to keep in the ordinary course of its business, which will be subject a variety of legislative and regulatory retention periods (which should be specifically related to control A.15.1.3, Protection of organizational records). Records that provide evidence of the effectiveness of the ISMS are of a different nature from those records that the ISMS exists to protect but, nevertheless, these records must, themselves, be controlled and must remain legible, readily identifiable and retrievable. This means that, particularly for electronic records, a means of accessing them must be retained even after hardware and software has been upgraded.

6.6 Documentation process and toolkits

The creation of the ISMS documentation is a key part of the process. It contains all the policies, procedures and records that set out how the ISMS should work and which record the evidence that it has worked. Organizations have two options about how they approach this, the most time-consuming part of the implementation:

- to design the documentation in-house;
- to purchase a ready-made documentation toolkit, one which contains pre-written templates that can be adapted by each organization to the needs of its own particular ISMS.

When looking at these toolkits on the web, check that they are more than simply a collection of hundreds of individual policies. They should contain a draft ISMS policy statement, ISMS manual (including the risk assessment methodology, risk treatment plan outline, etc), Statement of Applicability, and draft policies and procedures that are aligned with the structure and numbering of ISO 27001. You should be able to take a free trial before you purchase, so that you can confirm that it really does meet the detailed requirements of the Standard.

CHAPTER 7

Project team

An ISMS project will need an appropriately structured and resourced project team. This is common sense; it also reflects the requirements of Clause 5 of ISO/IEC 27001 as well as complying with the requirements of controls A.6.1.1 through to A.6.1.3.

7.1 Demonstrating management commitment

Clause 5.1 of ISO 27001(and control A.6.1.1) requires management to demonstrate its commitment to the 'establishment, implementation, operation, monitoring, review, maintenance and improvement of the ISMS' and goes on to list the specific steps that will provide that evidence:

- establishing the ISMS policy, which should be formally debated and signed off by the board or top management team;
- ensuring that ISMS objectives and plans are established, which is best done through the ISMS project team (see below);
- establishing roles and responsibilities for information security, which should start with establishing the ISMS project team;
- communicating the importance of information security to the organization and providing ongoing support for the ISMS and its continual improvement;
- providing sufficient resources for all stages and aspects of the ISMS development and deployment;
- deciding the risk acceptance and control criteria, which should be done at a formal management meeting;
- ensuring that the ISMS audits (as required under the 'Check' phase) are carried out;
- conducting management reviews of the ISMS (also as required under the 'Check' phase).

7.2 Project team/steering committee

Top management should create a business-led project team or steering committee to design and implement the ISMS. This team should be led by a senior manager with general business responsibility, ideally the CEO. Experience teaches that this team should not be led by an IT manager, as this IT managers don't tend to have sufficient cross-business and general management experience and credibility to create and implement a management system that has to work across the business as a whole.

The project team, led by a general manager, should include key functional managers as well as IT and information security technical expertise. Where the resources are not available in-house, this technical expertise should be externally contracted; where an external contractor is used, the various control requirements related to third party contracts, such as A.6.1.5, Confidentiality Agreements, and A.6.2, External Parties, should be applied.

7.3 Information security co-ordination

Control A.6.1.2 requires information security to be co-ordinated across the organization by representatives from different parts of the organization. In all but the largest organizations, this team should be the same team as the ISMS project team. This team can also be given the task of the detailed allocation of information security responsibilities that is envisaged by A.6.1.3, Allocation of Information Security Responsibilities.

The ideal ISMS project team is shown in Figure 7.1.

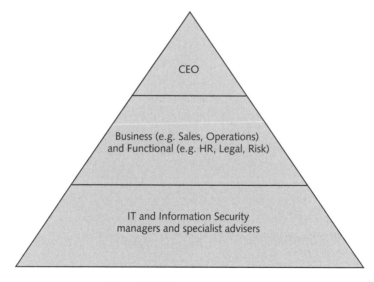

Figure 7.1 *ISMS project team structure*

CHAPTER 8

Project initiation

The preparatory, pre-project phase of an ISMS implementation should involve at least the following four stages:

- *awareness* - developing an understanding, amongst the board, senior management and key functional managers, of why an information security management system is required and, broadly, what is likely to be involved;
- *learning* - developing, in greater depth, the skills and knowledge of those likely to be in the project team and more directly involved in the project itself;
- *scoping* - determining what will be within the scope of the ISMS and what will be outside it;
- *policy formulation* - developing and agreeing the information security policy for the organization. This policy sets the direction for the ISMS within the context of the business objectives.

8.1 Awareness

Deploying an ISMS is a business project, not a technical or IT one.

Unless the ISMS project has the active support of the board, top management and those senior managers (business and functional) whose influence in the business is critical to the success of any project, it will fail.

ISO 27001, in Clause 5, also explicitly requires that management 'shall provide evidence of its commitment to the establishment, implementation, operation, monitoring, review, maintenance and improvement of the ISMS.' In the light of this, and of the explicit control and continuous improvement requirements described in the Standard, any organization that is developing and implementing an ISMS will make the full involvement of top management a priority. Clause 5 of the Standard - and the *Management Guide to ISO 27001 & ISO 27002* - support the argument that, without top management support, the organization simply will not be able to implement a useful ISMS, let alone achieve accredited certification.

8.2 Awareness tools

The most common methods of developing awareness are:
- circulation of copies of books such as this one to all who are likely to be involved;
- presentations and workshops, by internal or external experts, on the Standard and on the implementation requirements;
- use of e-learning or other internal communication and training tools;
- large scale staff presentations and training workshops.

It is important that all awareness-building exercises focus on the specific benefits the organization intends to derive from the implementation of an ISMS, and on the specific threats and risks faced by the organization, as this helps build understanding and commitment from all those staff members involved in the process.

CHAPTER 9

Process approach and the PDCA cycle

It is now expected that a 'process approach' will be applied to the design and deployment of an ISMS. This approach, widely know as the 'Plan-Do-Check-Act' (PDCA) model, is familiar to quality and business managers everywhere (figure 9.1).

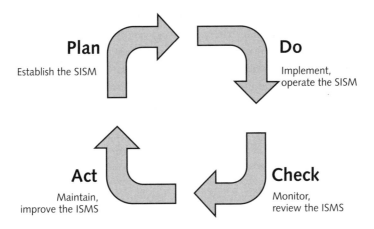

Plan
Establish the SISM

Do
Implement,
operate the SISM

Act
Maintain,
improve the ISMS

Check
Monitor,
review the ISMS

Figure 9.1 *PDCA model*

ISO 27001 identifies the PDCA model in Clause 0.2 and describes how to apply it in an information security environment. ISO 27001 'adopts the PDCA process model, which is applied to structure all ISMS processes.'[16] The PDCA approach should be thoroughly understood before work starts on designing and implementing an ISMS and should inform every step.

Application of the PDCA cycle to a process approach means that, following the basic principles of process design, there need to be both inputs to and outputs from the process. An ISMS takes, as its input, 'the information security requirements and expectations of the interested parties and through the necessary actions and processes produce information security outcomes that meets those requirements and expectations.'[17] This means that the PDCA model is applied at two levels:

---

14) ISO/IEC 27001:2005 0.2 Process approach
15) Ibid.

- at the strategic level, in terms of the overall development of the ISMS itself;
- at the tactical level, in terms of the development of each of the processes within the ISMS.

9.1 PDCA mapped to the clauses of ISO 27001

At the strategic level, the application of the PDCA cycle is applied to the development of the ISMS as described in the introduction. The correspondence between the PDCA cycle and the stages identified in the Standard for development of the ISMS is set out below.
Plan (Establish the ISMS, Clause 4.2.1):
- define the scope of the ISMS;
- define the information security policy;
- define a systematic approach to risk assessment;
- carry out a risk assessment to identify, within the context of the policy and ISMS scope, the important information assets of the organization and the risks to them;
- assess the risks;
- identify and evaluate options for the treatment of these risks;
- select, for each approach, the control objectives and controls to be implemented;
- prepare a Statement of Applicability (SoA).

Do (Implement and operate the ISMS, Clause 4.2.2):
- formulate the risk treatment plan, its documentation, including planned processes and detailed procedures;
- implement the risk treatment plan and planned controls;
- provide appropriate training for affected staff, as well as awareness programmes;
- manage operations and resources in line with the ISMS;
- implement procedures that enable prompt detection of, and response to, security incidents.

Check (Monitor and Review the ISMS, Clause 4.2.3):
- the 'check' stage has, essentially, only one step (or, set of steps): monitoring, reviewing, testing and audit;
- monitoring, reviewing, testing and audit is an ongoing process that has to cover the whole system and a certification body will want to see evidence of at least one cycle of tests and audits on the ISMS having been completed prior to a certification visit.

Act (Maintain and Improve the ISMS, Clause 4.2.4):

- testing and audit outcomes should be reviewed by management, as should the ISMS in the light of the changing risk environment, technology or other circumstances; improvements to the ISMS should be identified, documented and implemented;
- thereafter, it will be subject to ongoing review, further testing and improvement implementation, a process known as 'continuous improvement'.

9.2 ISMS project roadmap

Figure 10.1 shows a typical ISMS project roadmap based on the four PDCA stages. This roadmap only indicates the sequence of the tasks; it does not signify the relative amount of time that each will require.

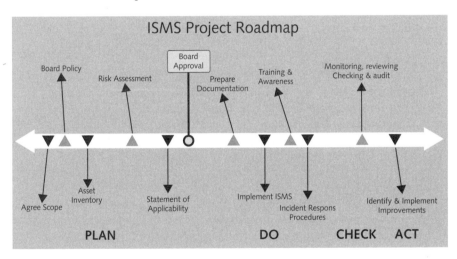

Figure 9.2 *ISMS project roadmap*

CHAPTER 10

Plan - establish the ISMS

The first phase of an ISMS project is covered in Clause 4.2.1 of ISO 27001. This is the longest individual clause in the Standard. Dealing correctly with the specification contained in this clause is foundational to the effective design, development and implementation of an ISMS that will really meet the requirements of the Standard.

10.1 ISMS policy

While the Standard's starting point relates to the scope of the ISMS, the real starting point is a board decision to pursue information security through a structured, coherent and managed process. The reason for this is that the ISMS cannot be scoped without a board policy decision on what it wants to protect, or why; the Standard requires that the ISMS reflects the business requirements. The policy, the requirement for which is set out in Clause 4.2.1.b, will be at the heart of the ISMS because it will contain the essential definitions, policies, responsibilities, requirements and expectations of the board in respect of the ISMS. It should be a precise, clear and rigorous document that provides firm and transparent guidance for the organization as it sets out to design and implement the ISMS.

This is also the first of many areas in which the specification contained in ISO 27001 is supported by the guidance and best practice of ISO 27002. Clause 5.1.1 of the latter matches the specification contained in Clause 4.2.1.b of ISO 27001. It explains that the control objective served by the issue of a policy document is that it provides 'management direction and support for information security in accordance with business requirements and relevant laws and regulation.'[18]

10.2 Policy and business objectives

Clause 5.1.1 goes on to state that the policy document should set a 'clear policy direction in line with business objectives'. Following this single piece of guidance can, for many organizations, be the single differentiator between designing and implementing a successful and useful ISMS and implementing something that undermines and blocks

---

18) ISO/IEC 27002:2005

business activity. The significant risk in implementing systems that block business activity, that are not (in the language of the Standard) in line with business objectives, is that people inside the business will ignore or bypass the ISMS controls 'in order to get something done'.

Policy is important, and drafting the policy so that every word is clear, unambiguous and meaningful may require a number of revisions of the initial drafts. However painstaking, the effort will make a real difference to the success of the ISMS. However, finalization of the policy is dependent on the completion of the scoping of the project. Scoping, one of the nine steps[19] to a successful ISO 27001 implementation, makes an essential contribution to the policy definition.

There are three other critical components of this first phase of an ISMS project. Apart from the scoping exercise (Clause 4.2.1. a), they are

- the risk assessment (Clauses 4.2.1 c, d, e, f and g);
- the risk treatment plan (Clause 4.2.2 a);
- the Statement of Applicability (Clause 4.2.1 j).

---

19) Nine Steps to Success: an ISO 27001 Implementation Overview (Alan Calder, ITG Publishing, 2005)

CHAPTER 11

Scope definition

The scoping requirement is contained in Clause 4.2.1 a), and is clearly meant to be seen as the first step in establishing an ISMS. The requirement of the organization that is contained within this clause is that it will 'define the scope and boundaries of the ISMS in terms of the characteristics of the business, the organization, its location, assets, technology, and including details of and justification for any exclusions from the scope.' Clause 1 (Scope) of the Standard should also be read (again) at this point. It makes clear that references to 'business' anywhere in the Standard 'should be interpreted broadly to mean those activities that are core to the purposes of the organization's existence.' This guidance is particularly valuable when attempting to consider intelligently the practical difficulty in developing an ISMS for only one part of any organization.

Clause 1 translates into four criteria that should be applied in deciding the scope of an ISMS project:

- What legal or management entity will be responsible and accountable for the ISMS?
- What information assets are owned, operated or depended upon by that entity?
- What processes are involved in manipulating, storing or sharing that information?
- What legal and regulatory requirements apply to that information (and in which jurisdictions)?

11.1 Scoping, boundaries and third party risk

A scoping exercise is designed to determine both what is within and what is without the ISMS. The ISMS will, in effect, erect a barrier between everything that is inside its perimeter and everything that is outside it. The development of the ISMS will require every point at which there is contact between the outside and the inside to be treated as a potential risk point, requiring specific and appropriate treatment. In particular, risk increases in direct proportion to the reduction in the organization's control over other parties. Figure 11.1 summarizes the risk aspects.

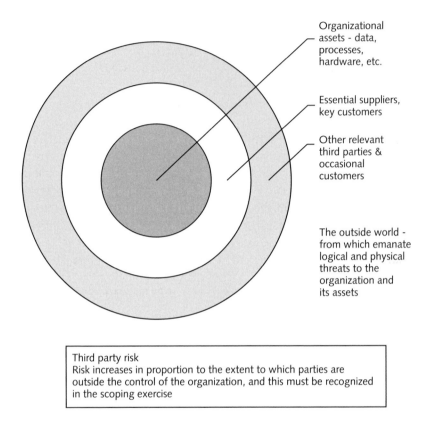

Organizational assets - data, processes, hardware, etc.

Essential suppliers, key customers

Other relevant third parties & occasional customers

The outside world - from which emanate logical and physical threats to the organization and its assets

Third party risk
Risk increases in proportion to the extent to which parties are outside the control of the organization, and this must be recognized in the scoping exercise

Figure 11.1 *Third party risk*

11.2 Scoping in small organizations

In smaller businesses, the decision about what should be within the scope of the information security policy is simple: everything. This is in line with the stated expectations of the Standard, which states that simple situations require simple solutions. ISO 27001's greater emphasis on the requirement that any exclusions from the scope should be specifically justified indicates an expectation that everything that is an information asset, or that has anything to do with an information asset, should be within the scope of the information security management system. This enables the management team to focus on a single system; integration with other process management systems is relatively straightforward. This principle should also apply in smaller organizations that have been required, either by a sector or regulatory scheme, or by the dictate of another organization, to achieve accredited certification in respect of a particular process. The practical difficulty of attempting to separate one process out from all the others in the organization is such that it is difficult to do in a way that will easily meet the requirements of the Standard.

11.3 Scoping in large organizations

In larger organizations, particularly those with multiple divisions, sites and operating units, the scoping decision is much more complex. The criteria identified above enable an appropriate decision to be made. Often, the simple act of listing all the information assets and information processes helps determine clearly the scope of the ISMS. The assets that are within scope will have to be the individual subject of risk assessments, so their early identification is advantageous to the project as a whole. Assets, like processes, cannot be half-in and half-out of the ISMS; they are either wholly in or wholly out, and the faster the organization is able to determine which, the better for the project as a whole.

11.4 Legal and regulatory frameworks

The legal and regulatory framework (4.2.1. b.2) also creates a specific perspective on the scoping of the ISMS for a larger organization. Clearly, information and information management processes that are all within the scope of any one single regulation or other legal requirement that is to be covered by the ISMS must all be within the scope of the ISMS.

11.5 Network infrastructure

Another perspective on the scoping exercise is by means of a network and a physical map (which must be 3-dimensional, in that it must also consider, for examples, floors and ceilings). It must be possible to identify clearly, on both maps, the secure perimeter created by and within which the ISMS is operative. All the assets and processes that are likely to be within the scope should be capable of being found on both these maps. If they are not, the maps will need to be re-drawn until the point at which all the relevant processes and assets are identified as being within a planned secure perimeter.

Network mapping (or topology) software can be used to create an effective and complete network map. A number of companies listed on Google offer free trials of their versions of this software. It is important, when creating such maps, to remember to include remote workers, mobile workers, wireless access points, and all the other components of today's 'porous perimeter'.

CHAPTER 12

Risk management

ISO 27001 requires (in Clause 4.2.1.b) the organization to take an explicitly risk-based approach to the selection and operation of information security controls.

Risk management is a discipline for dealing with non-speculative risks, those risks from which only a loss can occur. In other words, speculative risks can be seen as the subject of the organization's business strategy whereas non-speculative risks, which can reduce the value of the assets with which the organization undertakes its speculative business activity should be the subject of what the Standard calls a 'risk treatment plan'.

These non-speculative risks should be identified and plans made to deal with them ahead of their occurrence.

12.1 Risk treatment plans

Risk treatment plans have four, linked, objectives. These are to:
- eliminate risks (terminate them);
- reduce those that cannot be eliminated to 'acceptable' levels; (treat them);
- tolerate them, exercising carefully the controls that keep them 'acceptable';
- transfer them, by means of contract or insurance, to some other organization.

12.2 Acceptable risks

The definition of what is 'acceptable' is critical to any risk treatment plan, and the Standard requires management (in Clause 5.1 f) to 'decide the criteria for accepting risks and for acceptable risk levels.' Note that this is a management requirement. The auditor will want to see evidence of the process adopted by management to make these decisions, and will want to see how the decisions made in respect of information security risk fit 'within the context of the organization's overall business activities and the risks they face.'[20]

---

20) ISO/IEC 27001:2005 4.1 General requirements

12.3 Risk assessment

While ISO 27001 specifies the risk assessment steps that must be followed, ISO 17799:2005 provides substantial further guidance on the risk assessment but does not provide detailed guidance on how the assessment is to be conducted. Every organization has to choose the approach that is most applicable for its industry, complexity and risk environment. In its introduction, ISO 27002:2005 describes risk assessment in terms compatible with this Management Guide and refers the reader looking for more guidance to ISO 13335-3, which contains examples of risk assessment methodologies. This standard has now been replaced with ISO/IEC 27005, which provides substantial and useful guidance on information security risk assessment. ISO 27002 also adopts (from ISO Guide 73:2002) definitions of risk, risk analysis, risk assessment, risk evaluation, risk management and risk treatment. It is simplest if these definitions are, for the sake of consistency with the Standard and commonality of approach, adopted by any organization tackling risk management.

A risk treatment plan can only be drawn up once the assets within the scope of the ISMS - and the risks to their confidentiality, availability and integrity - have been identified, analyzed and assessed. Risk assessment is based on a data-gathering process and, as all individual inputs into the analysis will reflect individual prejudice, so the process of information gathering should question inputs to establish what really is known - and what is unknown.

The Standard sets out six steps that must be followed in carrying out a risk assessment:
- identify the assets within the scope of the ISMS;
- identify threats to the confidentiality, availability and integrity of those assets;
- identify the vulnerabilities those threats could exploit;
- assess the possible impacts of those threats;
- assess the likelihood of those events occurring;
- evaluate the risk.

CHAPTER 13

Assets within scope

The first step in the risk assessment process is (according to Clause (4.2.1.d1)) to identify all the information assets within the scope of the ISMS and, at the same time, to document which individual and/or department 'owns' the asset. An asset inventory is also a requirement of control A.7.1.1.

This exercise builds on, and could be part of, the scoping exercise. The key components of this exercise are:

- identifying the boundaries (physical and logical) of what is to be protected;
- identifying all the systems necessary for the reception, storage, manipulation and transmission of information or data within those boundaries and the information assets within those systems;
- identifying the relationships between these systems, the information assets and the organizational objectives and tasks;
- identifying the systems and information assets that are critical to the achievement of these organizational objectives and tasks and, if possible, ranking them in order of priority. Clause A.7.1 is the Annex A control that deals with the asset inventory and the guidance of Clause 7.1 of ISO 27002:2005 should be taken at this point. It identifies clearly the classes or types of information asset that should be considered, and recommends that the information security classification of the asset be determined at this time - which would be sensible, given the requirement of control A.7.2 for information is appropriately classified.

13.1 Asset classes

ISO 27002 identifies, in A.7.1.1, the six classes of assets that have to be considered. They are as follows:

- *information assets* include information printed or written on paper, transmitted by post or shown in films, or spoken in conversation, as well as information stored electronically on servers, web site(s), extranet(s), intranet(s), PCs, laptops, mobile phones and PDAs as well as on CD ROMs, floppy disks, USB sticks, back up tapes and any other digital or magnetic media, and information transmitted electronically by any means. It includes databases and data files, contacts and agreements, system documentation, research information, user manuals, training material, operational or support procedures, business continuity plans, fallback arrangements, audit trails, and archived information;

- *data* also includes the sets of instructions that tell the system(s) how to manipulate information (i.e. the software: operating systems, applications, development tools, utilities, etc);
- *physical assets* on which the information is manipulated: the computer and communications equipment (including, for instance, laptops, mobile phones, PDAs, etc), removable media (e.g. USB sticks, CD-ROMs, back-up tapes, etc);
- *services* on which computer systems depend: computing and communications services, and general utilities such as heating, lighting, power and air-conditioning. Burglar alarms might also be included;
- *people*, who carry much information in their heads, and the qualifications, skills and experience that is necessary for their interaction with the organization's data;
- *intangibles*, such as intellectual property, reputation, brand image, etc.

There should be a link between this inventory and the organization's fixed asset ledger, and the confidentiality classification (as required by clause 7 Annex A) of every asset, together with details of its owner, should be recorded as well.

13.2 Asset owners

ISO 27001 defines 'owner' as the 'individual or entity that has approved management responsibility for controlling the production, development, maintenance, use and security of the assets.'[21] Every asset must have an owner and this is contained in control requirement A.7.1.2 (ownership of assets). The owner of the asset is the person - or part of the business - who should be responsible for appropriate classification and protection of the asset. In real terms, allocating ownership to a part of the organization can be ineffective, unless that part has a clearly defined line of responsibility and accountability in place.

---

21) ISO/IEC 27001:2005 Footnote 2

CHAPTER 14

Assessing risk

Assets are subject to threats that exploit vulnerabilities; some threats are more likely than others, and every threat may have a unique impact. Risk assessment involves identifying all these aspects for every asset.

> Risk assessments - Key concept 1: *Threats exploit vulnerabilities*

14.1 Threats (4.2.1.d2)

These are things that can go wrong or that can 'attack' the identified assets. They can be either external or internal. Examples might include fire or fraud, virus or worm, hacker or terrorist. Threats are always present for every system or asset - because it is valuable to its owner, it will be valuable to someone else. You could assume that, if you cannot identify a threat to an asset, that it is not really an asset. So the next stage mandated by the Standard is to identify the potential threats to the systems and assets listed in compliance with A.7.1.1.

Identify, on an individual basis, threats to the confidentiality, integrity and availability of every asset within scope of the ISMS. You can do this through a brainstorming exercise or by using an appropriate threat database; technical expertise is essential if the threat identification step is to be carried out properly.

It is, of course, likely that an individual threat may appear against a number of assets but, crucially, the Standard requires the ISMS to be erected on the foundation of a detailed identification and assessment of the threats to each individual information asset that is within scope. From a practical point of view, if a number of assets fall within the same class and are exactly the same (e.g. desktop computers that have the same hardware specifications, software build, connectivity configuration and user exposure) they might be considered as a class of assets and the subsequent phases of this exercise could be carried out treating them on that basis. Where there is any doubt or uncertainty, however, resort to assessing threats on an individual asset basis.

14.2 Vulnerabilities (4.2.1.d3)

These leave a system open to attack by something that is classified as a threat or allow an attack to have some success or greater impact. For example, for the external threat of 'fire', a vulnerability could be the presence of inflammable materials (e.g. paper) in the server room. In the language of the Standard, a vulnerability can be exploited by a threat.

The next stage in the assessment process, therefore, is to identify - for every single one of the assets that you have identified and for each of the threats that you have listed alongside each of the assets, the vulnerabilities that each threat could exploit. Clearly, a single asset could face a number of threats, and each threat could exploit more than one vulnerability. You need to identify them all, and one way of doing this - particularly for computer hardware and software - is to refer to standard industry sources such as Bugraq and CVE. Any manufacturer's updates that identify vulnerabilities should be taken into account, as should the fact that not all vulnerabilities have, on any one day, yet been identified and, therefore, the organization will need to be able to identify new vulnerabilities as and when they occur. Of course, the working assumption in carrying out this stage of the exercise is that no controls are currently in place - there is, in other words, a certain 'what if?' element, as in 'what vulnerability does the operating system have to a Trojan threat?' Answer: 'Windows XP vulnerabilities to Trojan threats are listed (wherever you choose).'

14.3 Impacts (4.2.1.d4)

The successful exploitation of a vulnerability by a threat will have an impact on the asset's availability, confidentiality or integrity. A single threat could exploit more than one vulnerability and each exploitation could have more than one type of impact. These impacts should all be identified. Risk assessment involves identifying the potential business harm that might result from each of these identified impacts.

The way to do this is to assess the extent of the possible loss to the business for each potential impact. One object of this exercise is to priorities treatment (controls) and to do so in the context of the organization's acceptable risk threshold; it therefore makes sense to categories possible loss rather than attempt to calculate it exactly. A stepped set of monetary, financial levels (e.g. High-Medium-Low) should be designed that, under the board's guidance, are appropriate to the size of the organization and its current risk treatment framework. In assessing the potential costs of impact, all identifiable costs - direct, indirect and consequential - including the costs of being out of business - should be taken into account.

Risk assessments - Key concept 2: *Potential event impact determines exposure level*

14.4 Risk assessment (likelihood and evaluation) (4.2.1.e)

Practically speaking, the process until this point has been about data gathering and factual assessment. Each of the preceding stages has a relatively high degree of certainty about it. The vulnerabilities should be capable of technical, logical or physical identification. The way in which threats might exploit them should also be mechanically demonstrable. The decisions that have to be made are those that relate to the actions the organization will take to counter those threats. This means that the actual risks have now to be assessed and related to the organization's overall 'risk appetite' - that is, its willingness to take risks.

Until this point, the assessment has been carried out as though there was an equal likelihood of every identified threat actually happening. This is not really the case and this is therefore where there must be an assessment - for every identified impact - of the likelihood or probability of it actually occurring. Probabilities might range from 'not very likely' (e.g., major earthquake in Southern England destroying primary and backup facilities) to 'almost daily' (e.g. several hundred automated malware and hack attacks against the network). Again, a simple set of stepped levels should be used.

Risk assessments - Key concept 3: *Event likelihood prioritizes control action*

14.5 Risk level

Risk level is a function of impact and likelihood, or probability. The final step in this exercise is to assess the risk level for each impact and to transfer the details to the corporate asset and risk log. Three levels of risk assessment are usually adequate: low, medium and high. Where the likely impact is low and the probability is also low, then the risk level could be considered low. Where the impact is at least high and the probability is also at least high, then the risk level would be high; anything between these two measures would be classed as medium. However, every organization has to decide for itself what it wants to set as the thresholds for categorizing each potential impact and from time to time it may be helpful to have four or more risk levels (including one such as minimal) in order to better priorities actions.

Figure 14.1 is a simple risk level matrix. It shows that the risk events with a high likelihood of occurring, and a high impact when they do, are the high risks and should be given priority treatment.

	Impact			
Likeli-hood	High	High	Medium	Low
	High	Medium	Medium	Low
	Medium	Medium	Low	Minimal
	Medium	Low	Minimal	Minimal

Figure 14.1 *Simple risk level matrix*

CHAPTER 15
Risk treatment plan

Clause 4.2.2.a of the Standard requires the organization to 'formulate a risk treatment plan that identifies the appropriate management action, responsibilities and priorities for managing information security risks'. This clause also specifically cross-refers to clause 5, a substantial clause dealing in detail with management responsibility, and which was covered earlier in this pocket book.

The risk treatment plan must be documented. It should be set within the context of the organization's information security policy and it should clearly identify the organization's approach to risk and its criteria for accepting risk. These criteria should, where a risk treatment framework already exists, be consistent with the requirements of the Standard as well as with the criteria the organization uses for evaluation of all sorts of risk.

The risk assessment process must be formally defined and described and the responsibility for carrying it out, reviewing it and renewing it, formally allocated. At the heart of this plan is a detailed schedule, which shows, for each identified risk:

- the acceptable level of risk;
- the risk treatment option that will bring the risk within an acceptable level;
- how the organization has decided to treat it;
- what controls are already in place;
- what additional controls are considered necessary;
- the timeframe for implementing them.

The risk treatment plan links the risk assessment (detailed, as described in the previous chapter, in the corporate information asset and risk log) to the identification and design of appropriate controls, as described in the Statement of Applicability, such that the board's defined approach to risk is implemented, tested and improved. This plan should also ensure that there is adequate funding and resources for implementation of the selected controls and should set out clearly what these are.

The risk treatment plan should also identify the individual competence and broader training and awareness requirements necessary for its execution and continuous improvement.

The risk treatment plan is the key document that links all four phases of the PDCA cycle for the ISMS. It is a high-level, documented identification of who is responsible for delivering which risk management objectives, of how this is to be done, with what resources, and how this is to be assessed and improved. At its core, it is the detailed schedule describing who is responsible for taking what action, in respect of each risk, to bring it within board-defined acceptable levels. Table 15.1 shows an outline risk treatment plan.

Asset	Risk assessment	Control decision	Control requirement	Actual control	Gap	Action required	Account-ability
Name, owner, classification	High, medium, low, minimal	Accept, reject, transfer, control	E.g. Anti-malware software on desktop and gateway	E.g. Anti-malware software is on gateway only	No desktop anti-malware software	Select, purchase and deploy desktop version	Name, dates, budgets, dependencies

Table 15.1 *Outline risk treatment plan*

One also has to consider the risk treatment plan in two parts; the first part is originated during the plan phase and the second part is treated, within ISO 27001, as part of the 'Do' phase and is created after a gap analysis.

CHAPTER 16

Risk assessment tools

The risk assessment is a complex and data-rich process. For an organization of any size, the only practical way to carry it out is to create a database that contains details of all the assets within the scope of the ISMS, and then to link, to each asset, the details of its threats, vulnerabilities, impacts and their likelihood, together with details of the asset ownership and its confidentiality classification. The risk assessment process is made enormously simpler if one can also use pre-created databases of threats and vulnerabilities.

This database must be updated in the light of new risk assessments, which should take place whenever there are changes to the assets or to the risk environment.

The complexity of this task is such that many organizations want to use some form of automated tool to perform their risk assessment. It is worthwhile to be clear about what is - and what is not - a risk assessment tool.

16.1 Gap analysis tools

A gap analysis tool is not the same thing as an ISO27001-compliant risk assessment tool. A risk assessment is individual asset-based, whereas a gap analysis assesses the gap between the requirements of a standard or other set of requirements (such as a risk treatment plan or Statement of Applicability) and the controls that are actually in place.

Such gap analysis tools almost invariably analyze the gap between the controls in place in an organization and those required by the Standard. While this exercise can be interesting, it is not deeply useful. This is because, where ISO27002 is concerned, not all organizations are likely to need to implement all the controls identified in the Standard. An analysis of the gap between the requirements of the Standard and the current implementation status is not particularly useful in the creation of an ISO27001-compliant ISMS.

There is no point in attempting to use such a tool to carry out the risk assessment component of the ISMS project, because it simply does not meet the requirements of the Standard.

16.2 Vulnerability assessment tools

Vulnerability assessment tools, also called security scanning tools, are also not risk assessment tools as defined by the Standard. They do have a role to play in many information security management systems, and that role is determined by the risk treatment plan which arises from the risk assessment. Vulnerability assessment tools assess the security of network or host systems and report system vulnerabilities. These tools are automated and designed to scan networks, servers, firewalls, routers, and software applications for vulnerabilities. Generally, the tools can detect known security flaws or bugs in software and hardware, determine if the systems are susceptible to known attacks and exploits, and search for system vulnerabilities such as settings contrary to established security policies.

In evaluating a vulnerability assessment tool, consider how frequently it is updated to include the detection of new weaknesses, security flaws and bugs, and whether or not it refers to common lists of flaws and vulnerabilities such as:

- SANS Top Twenty (www.sans.org/top20);
- NIST (nvd.nist.gov);
- CVE (www.cve.mitre.org);
- Bugtraq (www.securityfocus.com/archive/1).

Vulnerability assessment tools are not usually run in real-time, but are commonly run on a periodic basis. The tools can generate both technical and management reports, including text, charts, and graphs. Vulnerability assessment reports can identify what weaknesses exist and how to fix them. Some tools automatically fix detected vulnerabilities.

16.3 Penetration testing

Penetration testing (or 'pentesting') is also not a risk assessment. A penetration analysis is a snapshot of the organization's security at a specific point in time. It can test the effectiveness of security controls and preparedness measures.

Penetration testing usually involves a team of (external) experts who test and identify an information system's vulnerability to attack. They may attempt to bypass security controls by exploiting identified vulnerabilities including, for instance, social engineering, denial of service attacks and other methods. The objective of a penetration analysis is to locate system vulnerabilities so that appropriate corrective steps can be taken.

The organization's risk treatment plan will determine whether or not penetration testing should form part of the organization's ISMS. The more extensive an organization's Internet exposure, the more important penetration testing is likely to be. Penetration testing should be carried out by someone who is independent of the managers responsible for the systems being tested and should be conducted by a trusted external organization, a qualified and experienced internal audit team, or a combination of both. The ISMS should prescribe the frequency and scope of the penetration testing and analysis. In determining the scope of the exercise, items to consider include:

- internal vs. external threats;
- which systems to include in the test;
- testing methods;
- system architectures.

16.4 Risk assessment tools

Risk assessment tools must meet the requirements of the Standard, otherwise there is no point in deploying them. This means that they must provide a meaningful facility for building an asset inventory in line with the requirements of A.7.1.1, and to record details of the asset owners and the asset classification. It must, in effect, automate the steps prescribed by the Standard.

4.2.1d:[22]

- Identify the assets within the scope of the ISMS, and the owners of these assets.
- Identify the threats to those assets
- Identify the vulnerabilities that might be exploited by the threats.
- Identify the impacts that losses of confidentiality, integrity and availability may have on the assets.

It must then identify (4.2.1e):
- the impact on the organization of the impact on each asset;
- the realistic likelihood of the occurrence of such an event;
- the level of risk for each event;
- whether or not the risk is acceptable or is to be controlled.

If the risk assessment tool does not work through these steps it is not worth having; any assessment produced by it will not meet the requirements of the Standard.

---

22) Excerpt from ISO/IEC 27001:2005. ISO/IEC 27002:2005 requirements are the same.

There are a number of practical, commercial considerations that should also be applied in considering the purchase of any risk assessment tool, including:

- the platform the tool is to run on (laptop, server, asp server, etc);
- *scalability* (to the needs of the organization and the number of users);
- *flexibility* - (the ability to divide the process into various sections and run them as discrete assessments in their own right. i.e. for business units, or for specific IT systems, or after change to an asset, and then the option to analyze wider impact in a full assessment);
- *import* (of, for instance, asset lists) and export facility;
- *extent* of *threat databases*;
- *customizable reporting* - for instance to suit organizational structures;
- *customizable questionnaires* - to suit evolving requirements;
- *license model* - single user may be the cost-effective option;
- *ease of use* - because the more training that is required, the higher the total cost of ownership, particularly when you provide for backup expertise;
- *price*.

16.5 Statement of Applicability

A risk assessment tool should also record the risk treatment decisions and generate, in its raw form, an ISO 27001-compliant Statement of Applicability.

CHAPTER 17

Statement of Applicability

The Statement of Applicability is central to an ISMS and to accredited certification of the ISMS (it is the document from which an auditor will begin the process of confirming whether or not appropriate controls are in place and operative). However, it can really only be prepared once the risk assessment has been completed and the risk treatment plan documented.

The Standard, at Clause 4.2.1.g, requires the organization to select appropriate control objectives and controls from those specified in Annex A, and requires the selection (and exclusion) of controls to be justified. Additional controls may also be selected, if those contained in Annex A are inadequate in the light of the risk assessment.

ISO 27001 auditors are likely to challenge implemented controls that are in excess of those required by the risk assessment on the basis that this may indicate inadequate controls applied elsewhere. ISO 27002 provides good practice on the purpose and implementation of each of the controls listed in Annex A. There are, however, some areas in which organizations may need to go further than is specified in ISO 27002; the extent to which this may be necessary is driven by the extent to which technology and threats have evolved since the finalization of ISO 27002:2005.

17.1 Controls (4.2.1.f.1)

Controls make up the bulk of the ISMS and implementing them will be the most resource-consuming part of the 'Do' phase. ISO 27002 is essentially a set of best-practice controls.

- Controls are responses to or countermeasures for risks.
- Controls reduce risks; they do not eliminate them.
- Controls should only be implemented in response to specific, identified risks.

Apart from knowingly accepting risks that fall within whatever criteria of acceptability the organization adopted in its risk treatment plan, or transferring the risk (through contract or insurance) to others, there are four types:

- deterrent controls reduce the likelihood of a deliberate attack;
- preventative controls protect vulnerabilities and make an attack unsuccessful or reduce its impact;
- corrective controls reduce the effect of an attack;
- detective controls discover attacks and trigger preventative or corrective controls.

Controls can be complex. Complex controls are a combination of technology, behavior and procedure. For instance, an anti-virus control is likely to consist of:
- anti-virus software installed on gateway and desktops (A.10.4.1);
- a documented procedure for ensuring regular software updates (A.10.1.1);
- training staff not to open unexpected attachments (A.8.2.2).

It is essential that any controls that are implemented are cost-effective. The principle is that the cost of implementing and maintaining a control should be no greater than the cost of the impact. This means that the cost of their implementation (in cash and resource deployment) should not exceed the potential impact (assessed in line with the guidance above) of the risks (including safety, personal information, legal and regulatory obligations, image and reputation) they are designed to reduce.

It is not possible or practical to provide total security against every single risk, but it is possible to provide effective security against most risks by controlling them to a level where the residual risk is acceptable to management. Risks can and do, however, change and so the process of reviewing and assessing risks and controls is an essential, ongoing one.

17.2 Controls and control objectives

Controls are selected in the light of a control objective. A control objective is a statement of an organization's intent to control some part of its processes or assets and what it intends to achieve through application of the control. One control objective may be served by a number of controls. ISO 27001 Annex A contains a comprehensive list of control objectives and controls that may achieve that objective.

It is important that, when considering controls, the likely security incidents that may need to be detected are considered and planned for. Clause 4.2.2.h of the Standard requires the implementation of controls that will enable 'prompt detection of and response to security incidents'. In effect, the process of selecting individual controls from those listed in the Standard's Annex A should include consideration of what evidence will be required, and what measurements of effectiveness (4.2.2.d) will be made to demonstrate that:
- the control has been implemented and is working effectively;
- each risk has thereby been reduced to an acceptable level, as required by clause 4.2.1 of the Standard. In other words, controls must be constructed in such a manner that any error, or failure during its execution, is capable of prompt detection and that

planned corrective action, whether automated or manual, is effective in reducing the risk of whatever may happen next to an acceptable level.

17.3 ISO 27001:2005 Annex A

ISO 27001:2005 Annex A has 11 major clauses or control areas numbered from A.5 to A.15, each of which identifies one or more control objectives. Control area A.6, organization of information security, for instance, has two control objectives: A.6.1 internal organization and A.6.2 external parties. Each control objective is served by one or more controls. Control objective A.5.1, information security policy, for instance, has two controls: A.5.1.1 information security policy document and A.5.1.2 review of the information security policy.

Every control is sequentially numbered. There are, in total, 133 sub clauses, each of which has a four-character alpha-numeric clause number. Each of these sub-clauses is an ISO 27001 control and each of them needs to be considered and a decision made as to whether or not it is applicable within the organization's ISMS.

As the controls are selected, the Statement of Applicability (SoA) can start being drawn up. This SoA, specified in 4.2.1.j of the Standard, is documentation of the decisions reached against the requirement to consider controls and is also an explanation or justification of why any controls that are listed in Annex A have not been selected. This document needs to be reviewed on a defined, regular basis and will be one of the first documents that the external auditor will want to see. It is also the document that is used to demonstrate to third parties the degree of security that has been implemented and is usually referred to, with its issue status, in the certificate of compliance issued by third party certification bodies.

Annex A is also aligned with ISO 27002:2005; this means that precisely the same control objectives, controls, clause numbering and wording are used in both Annex A and in ISO 27002. ISO 27002, however, provides substantial, detailed, technology-neutral and vendor-independent guidance on how to implement each of the controls and it is therefore an essential component of an ISO 27001 implementation. Note the clear statement that 'the lists in these tables are not exhaustive and an organization may consider that additional control objectives and controls are necessary.'[23]

---

23) ISO/IEC 27001:2005 Annex A Introduction

17.4 Drafting the Statement of Applicability

As indicated above, the Statement of Applicability is, essentially, a list of all the control objectives and controls that are contained in Annex A plus additional control objectives and controls that have been identified through the risk assessment process, or the requirements of a sector scheme, or both.

For each control objective and control, it identifies how that control has been applied by reference to a policy, procedure or instruction that describes precisely how the control is implemented. An excerpt from an organization's Statement of Applicability (which includes one control - 11.4.5 - that is not applied) is set out in table 17.1.

11.3.3 Clear desk and screen policy
The Organization has adopted a clear desk policy for papers and removable storage media and a clear screen policy for information processing facilities and the requirement for compliance with this policy is set out in DOC 11.4.
11.4 Network access control
Control objective: to prevent unauthorized access to networked services
11.4.1 Policy on use of network services
The Organization's policy (in DOC 11.7) is that users are only provided with access to the services that they have been specifically authorized to use.
11.4.2 User authentication for external connections
DOC 11.8 sets out the authentication methods that are used to control access by remote users
11.4.3 Equipment identification in the network
Automatic equipment identification is used as set out in DOC 11.8 as a means to authenticate connections from specific locations and equipment
11.4.4 Remote diagnostic and configuration port protection
Physical and logical access to diagnostic and configuration ports is controlled as required by DOC 11.8.
11.4.5 Segregation in networks
The organization only has one network and one group of users, all of whom need access to the same information; it therefore does not segregate its networks.

Table 17.1 *Excerpt from an organization's Statement of Applicability*

17.5 Excluded controls

Those controls that are not required are identified, in their natural sequence in the Statement of Applicability, as not applying and a justification for this is provided.

For instance, control A.12.5.5, outsourced software development, is not relevant to all those organizations that do not have software developed externally for them and the justification that is documented in the SoA for excluding this control might simply read: 'This control has been excluded as the organization does not have any software developed externally.' The certification auditor is then at liberty to confirm whether or not this is the case but, from the perspective of ISO 27001, the SoA will have complied with the requirements of the Standard.

Finally, the SoA must be a living document. It will not be adequate to create the SoA and then to leave it alone. The 'monitor, review, maintain and improve' requirements of clause 4.1 also apply to the SoA which should, on at least an annual basis or whenever there has been any significant change in the business or threat environment or in the information systems and assets of the organization, be reviewed to confirm that the controls are still applicable.

CHAPTER 18

Third party checklists and resources

Both ISO/IEC 27001 and ISO/IEC 27002 are relatively high level standards, in that they are deliberately technology-neutral. While they provide best practice, both in terms of the specification of an ISMS and the selection of information security controls, they do not provide specific guidance on what controls should be implemented in specific circumstances.

There are two potential sources for detailed hardware- and software-related information security controls. The first is the manufacturer of the hardware or software that is deployed in your organization, who should be able to provide information about the default security configuration of the software and hardware as it was supplied, together with recommendations as to appropriate security settings for specific deployments and usages of their products. This guidance should be considered in the light of a risk assessment carried out in line with the organizations risk assessment methodology and, if appropriate, it should be followed.

18.1 Third party sources

The second source for information is independent third party organizations such as ISACA, the ISF, SANS and others. In particular, the Computer Security Resource Center (www.csrc.nist.gov) of the US National Institute of Standards and Technology, which publishes a library of documents on computer security. This library includes its 800-series Special Publications which, since 1990, has contained NIST's 'research, guidance and outreach efforts in computer security, and its collaborative activities with industry, government and academic organizations.'

18.2 Configuration checklists

The library includes, for instance, a security checklist for securing Windows XP systems, and SP800-70 is NIST's special programme for security configuration checklists for IT products. A 'checklist' provides guidance on how to 'lock down' or 'harden' a specific computer item (hardware or software) to minimize its vulnerabilities in specific environments. 'Because IT products are often intended for a variety of audiences, restrictive security controls are usually not enabled by default, so many IT products are immediately vulnerable out-of-the-box. It is a complicated, arduous and time-consuming task for even experienced system administrators to identify a reasonable set of security settings for many IT products.'[24]

SP800-70 enables users to access checklists available from NIST, as well as providing guidance on how new checklists might be developed.

18.3 Vulnerability databases

The vast majority of computer vulnerabilities are widely known; however, new vulnerabilities are identified on a daily basis. Most information security threats exploit these widely known vulnerabilities. It makes sense for any organization that is implementing an ISMS to be aware of both known and evolving vulnerabilities and Nest's publicly available national vulnerability database (nvd.nist.gov) is a comprehensive database that integrates all publicly available US government vulnerability resources and which is updated on a daily basis, using standard definitions and providing a severity estimate. Other publicly available vulnerability databases are listed in Chapter 16.

---

24) SP800-70, page 9

CHAPTER 19

Do - implement and operate the ISMS

The first phase of implementing an ISMS concludes, according to ISO 27001, with the completion of the Statement of Applicability. This SoA must identify the control objectives and controls selected and the reasons for their selection, which points backwards to the risk assessment and the risk treatment criteria selected in the risk treatment plan. The Standard also requires an identification of the controls currently implemented (4.2.2.j.2), which is the essential precursor to carrying out a step that, while not specifically mandated within the Standard, is implied and is commonly understood to be the essential step before the next identified phase can be taken forward.

19.1 Gap analysis

The next practical step is to carry out a gap analysis, as shown in figure 19.1. The objective of the gap analysis is to determine the gap between the controls that the risk assessment process identified as required and which are documented in the SoA, and those controls that are actually in place. It is not uncommon, in most organizations, for the controls that are actually in place to be unaligned with those that are required. This lack of alignment is not only in terms of the absence of required controls; it is not unusual for an organization to discover that it has in place controls that do not need to operate the way that they do, or which are not needed at all. The gap analysis requires an assessment that deals with both the managerial and process aspects of the ISMS as well as the technical controls that have been implemented and is best carried out be experts who are independent of the areas being assessed.

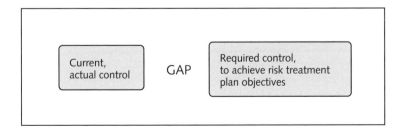

Figure 19.1 *Gap analysis*

This gap analysis enables the organization to put together the second and most important part of the risk treatment plan, the 'management action, resources, responsibilities and priorities for managing information security risks,'[25] which is the detailed set of actions (What? By whom? By When? Etc) that, between them, enable the organization to actually implement its ISMS. As described earlier, the risk treatment plan is the key document that links all four phases of the PDCA cycle for the ISMS and which ensures that everything that needs to be done is actually done.

19.2 Implementation

The rest of this second phase of the ISMS design and implementation contains five activities whose descriptions are deceptively simple:
- implement the risk treatment plan and the controls identified in the SoA (4.2.2.b and c);
- define how to measure and assess the effectiveness of all the controls (4.2.2.d);
- implement training and awareness programmes (4.2.2.e), which links to control A.8.2.2, information security awareness, education and training. To a very high degree, the success of the ISMS depends on individual behaviors; effective information security is always a combination of technology, individual behavior and process. One without the other is not particularly successful; for instance, while anti-virus software is responsible for automatically detecting and eliminating malware at the perimeter gateway, it will rapidly become ineffective if there is no standard process for updating it (every day), and its effectiveness will also potentially be undermined by any member of staff who uploads files from a third party's USB stick or who opens an unsolicited incoming .exe email attachment. Management needs to ensure that it has in place a wide ranging and comprehensive awareness and training programme that brings everyone's knowledge up to a minimum adequate level, inducts new members of the team, and keeps everyone up-to-date with most recent threats, risks and avoidance techniques. Of course, employees need to be sufficiently motivated to address the issue in the first place and this is why the commitment, enthusiasm and leadership of top management is so crucial;
- manage the ISMS (4.2.2.f and g); day-to-day management of the ISMS should be straightforward, but it is not. All the interlocking controls and processes must be kept working, new threats identified, evaluated and, if necessary, neutralized. People must be recruited and trained, their performance supervised and rewarded (or not,

---

25) ISO/IEC 27001:2005 4.2.2.a

as the case may be), and their skills developed in line with the changing needs of the business. The effectiveness of the ISMS must be managed and its long term, continuous improvement planned and led;

- implement an incident detection and response procedure (4.2.2.h), the overall importance of which is indicated by the fact that it links to a clause that was introduced, for the first time at the highest level, in ISO 27002:2005, which is clause 13, information security incident management. This clause contains two control objectives and five controls. The development and implementation of an information security incident management process that conforms to the requirements of the Standard could always begin at the same time as the ISMS project itself starts up; the information gathered through this process can be invaluable in planning the ISMS itself.

CHAPTER 20

Check - monitor and review the ISMS

Clause 4.2.3 of the Standard is all about monitoring and review. It reflects strongly the requirement that management is actively involved in the long-term management of the ISMS while recognizing the reality that the information security threat environment changes even more quickly than the business environment. This clause deals, broadly, with three types of activity: monitoring, reviewing and auditing.

The purpose of monitoring activity is primarily to detect processing errors and information security events quickly so that immediate corrective action can be taken. Monitoring should be formal, systematic and widespread. Control area A.13, information security incident management, has at its heart the notion that the organization must monitor for deviations and incidents, respond to them and learn from them.

20.1 Audits

Audits, on the other hand, are specifically designed and planned to ensure that the controls documented in the SoA are effective and being applied, and to identify non-conformances and opportunities for improvement. Control objective A15.2 (Compliance with security policies and standards, and technical compliance checking) deals specifically with this issue and mandates regular, planned compliance reviews at both the process and the technical levels. This requirement is described in more depth in clause 6 of the Standard, which lays out two important aspects of this process. The first is that the audit programme 'shall be planned, taking into consideration the status and importance of the processes and areas to be audited, as well as the results of previous audits.'[26]

20.2 Audit programme

The audit programme plan should be risk based, and those areas of the ISMS that are exposed to the highest level of risk, or on which the organization has the highest degree of dependency, should be audited more regularly and in greater depth than less important areas. The audit programme should also take into account changes to

---

26) ISO/IEC 27001:2005, Clause 6a

the risk environment as well as to the ISMS and the business itself. Auditors should be appropriately trained and have suitable knowledge and experience.

The second important requirement is that 'the management responsible for the area being audited shall ensure that actions are taken without undue delay to eliminate detected non-conformities and their causes.'[27]

20.3 Reviews

Reviews of internal and external audits policies performance reports, exception reports, risk assessment reports and all the associated policies and procedures. are undertaken to ensure that the ISMS is continuing to be effective within its changing context.

There is, of course, a close interaction between the three elements of this stage and a number of the controls in Annex A and ISO 27002. The Annex A controls that are directly relevant to this stage of the ISMS PDCA cycle are:

- A.5.1.2 Review of the Information Security Policy;
- A.5.1.8 Independent review of information security;
- A.10.2.2 Monitoring and review of third party services;
- A.10.10 Monitoring is a single control objective that is related, obviously, to monitoring, and which contains 6 controls;
- A.11.2.4 Review of user access rights;
- A.12.2 Correct processing in applications is a control objective that in effect deals with monitoring application use and data processing;
- A.13.2.2 Learning from information security incidents;
- A.14.1.5 Testing, maintaining and re-assessing business continuity plans.

All these controls must be addressed in this third phase of the ISMS development and implementation. The findings and outcomes of the monitoring and reporting activity must be translated into corrective or improvement action and, for the purposes of the ISMS, the audit trail that demonstrates the decision making process and the implementation of those decisions should be retained in the ISMS records.

---

27) Ibid. Again, the Standard is clear that management at all levels of the organization has a role to play in the effective implementation, maintenance and improvement of the ISMS, and this should be taken into account in managerial and supervisory job descriptions, employment contracts, induction and other training, and performance reviews.

CHAPTER 21

Act - maintain and improve the ISMS

This chapter reflects the brief requirements of section 4.2.4 of ISO 27001. This clause sets out the requirement that everything learned through the monitoring and reviewing activity discussed in the previous chapter should be implemented. It also links to section 8 of the Standard, whose three clauses (8.1, continual improvement; 8.2, corrective action and 8.3, preventative action) specify the nature and purpose of the activity that must be part and parcel of the day-to-day activity of everyone involved in the day-to-day management of the ISMS.

21.1 Management review

In this context, this section also links to section 7, which deals with management review of the ISMS, and which stresses that this management review should take into account the 'status of preventative and corrective actions,'[28] as well as any changes anywhere or to anything that might affect the ISMS, and recommendations for improvement. Of course, this does mean that there needs to be a mechanism for collecting improvement recommendations. The requirement to take corrective and preventative action, and to seek continuous improvement, should not only be written into employment contracts, but could also be the subject of a long-term incentive and reward scheme.

It should be noted that corrective and preventative action should be prioritized on the basis of a risk assessment.[29] Assessing and evaluating risks is a core competence required in any organization that is serious about achieving and maintaining ISO 27001 accredited certification and the final sentence of the Standard, which makes the point that the prevention 'of non-conformities is often more cost-effective than corrective action,' sums up the risk-based, cost-effective, common-sense approach of the Standard.

---

28) ISO/IEC 27001:2005 7.2.d
29) IOS/IEC 27001:2005 8.3

CHAPTER 22

Measurement

In comparison to BS 7799-2:2002, ISO/IEC 27001:2005 provided a significantly increased emphasis on measurement. An ISO ISMS Measurements and Metrics Standard (ISO/IEC 27004) is currently under development.

Clause 4.2.2.d requires the organization to 'define how to measure the effectiveness of the selected controls or groups of controls and specify how these measurements are to be used to assess control effectiveness to produce comparable and reproducible results' and, in 4.2.3.c, to 'measure the effectiveness of controls to verify that security requirements have been met.'

These measurements should enable information security activity to be objectively analyzed and for the levels of information security actually achieved to be monitored over a period of time, as well as so that different organizations (or organizational divisions) can benchmark and compare information security effectiveness.

22.1 NIST SP800-55

The US National Institute of Standards and Technology publishes (at www.csrc.nist.gov) a series of information security guides and checklists. Guide 55, Security Metrics Guide for Information Technology Systems, provides 'guidance on how an organization, through the use of metrics, identifies the adequacy of in-place security controls, policies and procedures. It provides an approach to help management decide where to invest in additional security protection resources or identify and evaluate non-productive controls. It explains the metric development and implementation process and how it can also be used to adequately justify security control investments.'

Until the publication of ISO/IEC 27004, the NIST publication (which can be freely downloaded from www.csrc.nist.gov/publications/nistpubs/800-55/sp800-55.pdf) should be studied for guidance on the development of effective information security metrics.

CHAPTER 23

Preparing for an ISMS audit

It is essential to carry out a comprehensive review of the design and implementation of the ISMS before agreeing the date at which an external certification auditor should begin an accredited certification audit.

This review should be carried out by the organization's internal ISMS audit team - those who are already responsible for the audit activity mandated under clause 6 of ISO/IEC 27001. A comprehensive, step-by-step review is necessary, not only because it is a good way to ensure that nothing that might endanger the planned certification might have been missed, but because it is the best way of ensuring that the ISMS has been properly and completely implemented.

The review process should be documented as one of the reviews required under clause 6 and, once the detailed audit has been completed, management should review the findings and this review should be documented under the requirements of clause 7 of ISO/IEC 27001.

The most useful tool to use in carrying out this review is the workbook titled: Are you Ready for an ISMS Audit based on ISO/IEC 27001? This book works through the requirements of Clauses 4 - 8 of the Standard as well as of all the controls listed in Annex A and poses questions of the sort that a certification auditor will ask and which will ensure that all aspects of the Standard have been appropriately considered and implemented.

Bibliography of related standards, guides and books

Both ISO 27001 and ISO 27002 include extensive bibliographies of standards that may be relevant to the Standard. I am not going to repeat those lists here. The essential documents, without which no-one should attempt an ISMS implementation, and which should be available online through national standards bodies and other licensed distributors are:

- ISO/IEC 27001:2005 Information technology - security techniques - information security management systems - requirements;
- ISO/IEC 27002:2005 Information technology - security techniques - Code of practice for information security management.

The following documents are all identified as being helpful, but are not mandatory:

- ISO/IEC 20000-1:2005 IT Service management - specification for service management;
- ISO/IEC 20000-2:2005 IT Service Management - code of practice for service management;
- BS25999 - Two part standard for business continuity management;
- ITIL V3 Complete Lifecycle Publication Suite
- ISO 9001:2008 Quality management systems - requirements;
- CobiT (version 4.1)

The BSI Business Information Guides, available from BSI and BSI distributors:

- BIP 0071 Guidelines on requirements and preparation for ISMS certification based on ISO/IEC 27001;
- BIP 0072 Are you ready for an ISMS audit based on ISO/IEC 27001?
- BIP 0073 Guide to the implementation and auditing of ISMS controls based on ISO/IEC 27001;
- BIP 0074 Measuring the effectiveness of your ISMS implementations based on ISO/IEC 27001.

Books by Alan Calder:
- IT Governance: a Manager's Guide to Data Security and ISO27001/ISO27002, 4th edition (with Steve Watkins);
- The Case for ISO 27001;
- Nine Steps to Success: an ISO 27001 Implementation Overview.
- Information Security Risk Management for ISO27001 (with Steve Watkins)

Accredited certification and other bodies

United Kingdom Accreditation Service: .... www.ukas.com
Quality Register at TSO: .... www.quality-register.co.uk
Institute for Internal Auditors: .... www.theiia.org/itaudit
Institute of Quality Assurance: .... www.iqa.org
International Accreditation Forum: .... www.iaf.nu
International Auditor and Training Certification Association: .... www.iatca.org
International Register of Certificated Auditors .... www.irca.org
International Standards Organization: .... www.iso.ch
BSI: .... www.bsi-global.com
Bureau Veritas Quality International (BVQI): .... www.bvqi.com
DNV Certification Ltd: .... www.dnv.com
Lloyd's Register Quality Assurance Ltd (LRQA): .... www.lrqa.com
National Quality Assurance Ltd (NQA): .... www.nqa.com
SGS Yarsley: .... www.sgs.com
Information assurance (UK public sector): .... www.cabinetoffice.gov.uk/csia

ITIL Books

Van Haren
PUBLISHING

Foundations of IT Service Management Based on ITIL®V3

Now updated to encompass all of the implications of the V3 refresh of ITIL, the new V3 Foundations book looks at Best Practices, focusing on the Lifecycle approach, and covering the ITIL Service Lifecycle, processes and functions for Service Strategy, Service Design, Service Operation, Service Transition and Continual Service Improvement.

English €39.95 excl tax

ISBN 978 90 8753 057 0 (english edition)

Foundations of IT Service Management Based on ITIL®

The bestselling ITIL® V2 edition of this popular guide is available as usual, with 13 language options to give you the widest possible global perspective on this important subject.

English €39.95 excl tax

ISBN 978 90 77212 58 5 (english edition)

IT Service Management Based on ITIL®V3: A Pocket Guide

A concise summary for ITIL®V3, providing a quick and portable reference tool to this leading set of best practices for IT Service Management.

English €11.95 excl tax

ISBN 978 90 8753 102 7 (english edition)